I0517658

YOUR PEACE IS A PRIORITY

YOUR PEACE IS A PRIORITY

A DEVOTIONAL JOURNAL

DR. KIENA S. HUGHLEY

J MERRILL

J MERRILL

Copyright © 2025 J Merrill Publishing, Inc.

All rights reserved. No part of this publication may be reproduced, distributed, or transmitted in any form or by any means, including photocopying, recording, or other electronic or mechanical methods, without the prior written permission of the publisher, except for brief quotations in critical reviews and certain other noncommercial uses permitted by copyright law.

For permission requests, please contact the Permissions Coordinator at:

J Merrill Publishing, Inc.
434 Hillpine Drive
Columbus, OH 43207
www.JMerrill.pub

Library of Congress Control Number: *2025911290*
Paperback ISBN-13: *978-1-961475-45-8*
eBook ISBN-13: *978-1-961475-46-5*

Book Title: Your Peace is a Priority: A Devotional Journal
Author: *Dr. Kiena S. Hughley*

To my "trues," who give me grace: I thank you for allowing me to be me. I love you endlessly.

To my bishop and pastor: keep teaching. I'm listening and learning.

To my bestie: you are the most selfless person I know. May God continue to bless you.

To my mom and pops: thank you for your endless support and love.

My God, my God! You have been so good to me!

CONTENTS

FOREWORD
ARMINA NEWTON

"Lord my God, I called to you for help, and you healed me."

— PSALM 30:2 (NIV)

I have had the pleasure of knowing Dr. Hughley for over ten years now. She has been a dear friend and prayer partner whose words and feedback I cherish. Sometimes it would be me reaching out, asking for prayer, but there were also instances when she would reach out to me, being led by the Holy Spirit, sending a prayer or an encouraging word. I say "led by the Holy Spirit" because there could have been no other way she would have known to use such specific words, relating to what I was going through at a given time, as I am not a big sharer.

The journey to finding peace may require self-reflection, vulnerability, and allowing yourself to feel. It also requires you to seek help. This is why this book is so powerful and necessary. Dr. Hughley has provided encouragement, prayer, and tools to not only overcome what we may deal with in everyday life, but to discover peace in the process.

Since I have known Dr. Hughley, she has been insightful and uplifting, while allowing God to direct her path. The true beauty of her is her love of God and her devotion to Him and to ministry: praying first, seeking His guidance, and carrying out what He has placed on her heart. I believe this series of messages embodies all that she is. This collection was written to aid in your process, providing wisdom, scripture, and prayer as you seek a peace beyond your understanding—a journey that may take time, but trust the process . . . this journey is yours.

PREFACE
ARMINA NEWTON

I read an article by Victoria Maxwell, titled *"The 6 Steps of Healing You Need to Know,"* where the author listed the following steps in the healing process, which led to my journey to find peace: acceptance, insight, action, self-esteem, healing, and meaning. I have had my share of moments where I have gone through the steps of healing many times. From feeling defeated after divorce to feeling less than as a single mother of two, there were so many times when I felt I did not measure up to someone else's standard—or my own.

At first, I did not allow myself to be vulnerable because I thought I was too strong, that I could handle anything (denial). Then I found myself in my room for two days: no lights, no TV, no food, and limited interaction. I was broken. I cried out to God, saying, "Please help me!" and eventually sought out therapy. Through that process, I learned that I had gone through what was called a depressive episode. My first thought was, *How did I get here? How did I get so overwhelmed* (acceptance)?

I then took a long look at myself and realized I had burnt myself out (insight). This led to taking an introspective look at what was on my plate in order to shift things around according to importance, or get rid of things—or habits—that no longer served a purpose (action). I was also able to see that my spiritual life needed a makeover. Once I began to make the shift and pray diligently, I felt more like myself (self-esteem). I was able to make better decisions and focus, realizing I could only do so much, as I was only one person (healing).

Everything I had gone through allowed me to see that it is okay to not have all of the answers. There is life after what I thought was me being broken, which I now refer to as being *bruised*—because it did not break me. I now feel that I am at peace. Glory to God!

"And the peace of God, which passeth all understanding,
shall keep your hearts and minds through Christ Jesus."

— PHILIPPIANS 4:7 (KJV)

ABOUT THIS BOOK

It has taken me about two and a half years to complete this devotional. I began writing it after the height of the COVID pandemic. I had recently undergone major surgery and was recovering. Also during this time, I preached my first sermon and completed my doctorate. I had so much clarity—and dare I say it—peace. I left one place of employment, where I did not feel supported, for a promotion with an opportunity to lead and support others. I sold a home that I had known for almost sixteen years and purchased a new one. New beginnings. Things were going well. I was determined to complete this book. I would take my manuscript on vacation and do some editing, and I made a lot of progress.

However, by the time I entered the second year at my new place of employment, I can honestly say that I was beginning to lose my peace. *Hey, Peace! Where are you?* A combination of personal loss and professional stress were the top contributors.

If anyone ever questions how you grieve or process stress, it is okay to give them the side-eye. Grieving is not just about losing a loved one—but we all know that, right? Grief may, at times, ebb and flow between sadness and depression, laughter and smiles. And while this devotional is not about grief and how to "get through it," it is about finding peace in the midst of a storm and coming out on the other side, victorious!

This book is written in three parts. Like all stories, there is a beginning, middle, and end. This book is no different. In the first section, you will begin to unpack those things that are disrupting your peace. You will be guided through scripture, daily thoughts, and prayer starters. The middle of the book allows you to take an inward look at yourself. The Bible tells us to examine ourselves: *"Examine yourselves, whether ye be in the faith; prove your own selves"* (2 Corinthians 13:5, KJV). You will be directed to apply the scripture to your daily life and pray about it.

The final section reminds you that you are never alone in this journey and that He hears your prayers. The journey to peace is a process. You must trust Him and have faith to be transformed into what He wants you to be. You will be guided to uncover the underlying causes of why your peace is—or has been—disturbed, rather than just addressing the symptoms.

Renewing Mind, Body, and Soul in a Time of Uncertainty

During these times, some "church folk" referred to what is going on as the end of days, but to the unchurched or unlearned, it is another day in the struggle—and to them, it has just gotten more difficult.

So, what do you do in a time of need, a time of desperation, a time of uncertainty?

The Bible tells us, *"We are troubled on every side, yet not distressed; we are perplexed, but not in despair"* (2 Corinthians 4:8, KJV). In short, we are a resilient people!

It is time for a rebirth—a renewing of the mind, body, and soul. Are you ready? Let's get started!

RENEWING MIND, BODY & SOUL IN A TIME OF UNCERTAINTY

Renewing of the Mind

Daily Thought: *What you allow to occupy your mind will sooner or later determine your speech and/or actions.*

- First, declutter your area—your office space, car, and rooms in your house. Having a free-flowing space void of clutter opens your mind to think clearly and creatively.
- Second, speak positive affirmations or self-talk when you wake, throughout the day as needed, and before bed.
- Next, create a vision board or goal sheet to keep you focused and driven.
- Finally, refresh and/or update your résumé or create a business plan for that hobby you have always wanted to parlay into a business.

Renewing of the Body

Daily Thought: *My body is a temple and not a junk drawer.*

How many of us have that drawer that holds everything? You can find almost anything! What's the problem with that, you say? Glad you asked. Let's say that you have a utensil divider, so all of your utensils are there, but you begin to use the drawer as a catchall. Now everything is mixed up and spilling over into other areas. Your drawer is no longer used for its intended purpose. Each time it is opened, things are moved around, shifted, and more things are added. Now you have a difficult time closing it, so you begin stuffing things as you are trying to shut it. Been there, right? Tight fit?

Do you see where I'm going? We are what we eat and drink. I'm not saying not to indulge—I'm saying try not to overindulge.

- Overeating is like carrying extra luggage by yourself: it's heavy, makes you tired, and is not easily manageable.
- Repurpose your food—those veggies you are chopping for a salad? Take the end pieces and boil them to use as vegetable broth. Freeze it for later use. Now you have a broth with less salt and no preservatives. That fruit you are cutting for the kids? Add it to a smoothie with the leftover salad mix. (We know someone always leaves just a little in the bag—not enough for a full salad.)
- Finally, get up and move! Turn on some music and dance. Add some jumping jacks. Remember that decluttering? You have just gotten in some cardio!

Renewing of the Soul

Daily Thought: *Little by little, God will bless you. Having a breakthrough is a process, not a quick fix!*

Just as what we physically put into our bodies is important, our spiritual food is just as important. Grandma, MaDear, and Big Mama always made the best food on Sunday—that after-church food! It's called that because it makes you feel good: confident, loved. I know a man named Jesus who is the best soul food chef. He will feed you every day. You will never go hungry or thirsty.

How can you sit at His table? Glad you asked! Let's start simple.

- Along with those daily affirmations, give thanks.
- As you self-talk, start a conversation with Him.
- Remember that vision board and goal sheet? *"And the Lord answered me, and said, Write the vision, and make it plain upon tables, that he may run that readeth it. For the vision is yet for an appointed time, but at the end it shall speak, and not lie: though it tarry, wait for it; because it will surely come, it will not tarry"* (Habakkuk 2:2–3, KJV).
- Jeremiah 29:11 reminds us, *"For I know the thoughts that I think toward you, saith the Lord, thoughts of peace, and not of evil, to give you an expected end"* (KJV).

There are so many things happening in the world today. With all that is wrong, there are days when it feels like there is no silver lining. It's hard enough sometimes to deal with negative self-talk. It is very important that we do not oversaturate ourselves with negative images, negative messages, and negative people. We have to take "brain breaks" and self-care moments.

Things I Do to Stay Positive

Turn off the negative self-talk. We may do something wrong and then talk to ourselves about how we should have done it differently, or make decisions that turn out not to be the greatest. When you give in to negative self-talk, you make room for the enemy to occupy your mind. You invite unnecessary stress, fixation, and irritability. Forgive yourself and others—and keep it moving. Don't hold on to it.

Keep my circle tight/accountability partners. I try to surround myself with positive people—movers and shakers, people with vision. We all have times when we need to vent to someone, but don't be a complainer.

Create. Pick up a hobby that allows your creative side to take hold, something that takes your mind off daily stresses. For me, it's making candles, traveling, and baking.

Disconnect. Take a break from social media and work computers. I disconnect by watching movies and binge-watching Hulu and Netflix —and going to church on Sundays.

Ignore. I ignore the "noise." Certain scriptures help me to do that:

> *"Finally, brethren, whatsoever things are true, whatsoever things are honest, whatsoever things are just, whatsoever things are pure, whatsoever things are lovely, whatsoever things are of good report; if there be any virtue, and if there be any praise, think on these things"*

> — PHILIPPIANS 4:8, KJV

*"No weapon that is formed against thee shall prosper; and
every tongue that shall rise against thee in judgment
thou shalt condemn"*

— ISAIAH 54:17, KJV

We must stay connected to the Source.

DAY 1

Scripture(s):

> *"The way of peace they have not known; and there is no judgment in their goings: they have made them crooked paths: whosoever goeth therein shall not know peace."*
>
> — ISAIAH 59:8, KJV

> *"Be careful for nothing; but in every thing by prayer and supplication with thanksgiving let your requests be made known unto God. And the peace of God, which passeth all understanding, shall keep your hearts and minds through Christ Jesus."*
>
> — PHILIPPIANS 4:6–7, KJV

Daily Thought:

What you allow to occupy your mind will sooner or later determine your speech or actions.

_____
_____
_____
_____

Prayer Starter:

Father God, I pray that at the end of these thirty days, I will have peace, a greater prayer life, and a greater understanding of the promises You have for me. Teach me how to apply Your Word to my daily life. Help me to create a peaceful space around me. Guard and guide my words. Let them be kind to myself and to others.

Your Prayer:

Write your prayer here.

_____
_____
_____
_____
_____

DAY 2

Scripture(s):

> "The Lord is not slack concerning his promise, as some men
> count slackness; but is longsuffering to us-ward, not
> willing that any should perish, but that all should come
> to repentance."
>
> — 2 PETER 3:9, KJV

Daily Thought:

*Little by little, God will bless us. Having a breakthrough is a process, not a
quick fix.*

Prayer Starter:

Father God, thank You for Your Word of promise today. Thank You
for the opportunity to praise Your name. Lord, I pray that I
communicate better. I pray that I treat everyone kindly, despite how
they treat me. I want to be a blessing to others.

. . .

Your Prayer:

Write your prayer here.

_____

_____

_____

_____

_____

Reflection Prompt:

What is one thing you want to accomplish today?

_____

_____

_____

_____

_____

DAY 3

Scripture(s):

"And the Lord, he it is that doth go before thee; he will be with thee, he will not fail thee, neither forsake thee: fear not, neither be dismayed."

— (DEUTERONOMY 31:8, KJV)

Daily Thought:

Be watchful and pray. Know those who can and will support you in your time of need. There are situations and storms that you can get through and out of alone, but your strength can only take you so far. You need the unlimited strength of God to see you through.

Prayer Starter:

Thank You, Father, for this day. Help me choose my circle wisely and carefully. Thank You for allowing me to see people for who they are in my life. Father God, I pray for better relationships, confidence, discernment, and peace with all those I come into contact with.

Your Prayer:

Write your prayer here.

_____

_____

_____

_____

_____

DAY 4

Scripture(s):

"I say the truth in Christ, I lie not, my conscience also bearing me witness in the Holy Ghost." (Romans 9:1, KJV)

"These are the things that ye shall do; Speak ye every man the truth to his neighbour; execute the judgment of truth and peace in your gates: and let none of you imagine evil in your hearts against his neighbour; and love no false oath: for all these are things that I hate, saith the Lord." (Zechariah 8:16–17, KJV)

Daily Thought:

Speak the truth.

Prayer Starter:

Father God, I pray that You would continue to guide my words and thoughts. Help me to say exactly what is on my mind, but to do so in a way that is pleasing to You. Lord, I pray for peace in my mind and heart. Lead and guide me.

. . .

Your Prayer:

Write your prayer here.

_____

_____

_____

_____

_____

Reflection Prompt:

Who is one person you need to forgive?

_____

_____

_____

_____

_____

DAY 5

Scripture(s):

"Trust in the Lord with all thine heart; and lean not unto thine own understanding. In all thy ways acknowledge him, and he shall direct thy paths." (Proverbs 3:5–6, KJV)

"This I say then, Walk in the Spirit, and ye shall not fulfil the lust of the flesh." (Galatians 5:16, KJV)

"If we live in the Spirit, let us also walk in the Spirit." (Galatians 5:25, KJV)

Daily Thought:

Always seek God's insight before making a move.

Prayer Starter:

Lord, guide my steps. Let Your will be done in my relationships, both personal and professional, as well as in all matters of my life. Help me to be courageous and confident.

. . .

Your Prayer:

Write your prayer here.

_____

_____

_____

_____

_____

DAY 6

Scripture(s):

"If any of you lack wisdom, let him ask of God, that giveth to all men liberally, and upbraideth not; and it shall be given him." (James 1:5, KJV)

Daily Thought:

Wisdom and understanding are keys to good decision-making.

Prayer Starter:

Lord, I thank You for the time that I have been able to spend with You. I thank You for Your Word. Help me to apply what I have read to my daily life. I want to use the knowledge and experience gained to make better decisions. I pray for the wisdom to discern situations that cause me angst and uneasiness.

Your Prayer:

Write your prayer here.

Reflection Prompt:

What disturbs your peace?

DAY 7

Scripture(s):

"Confess your faults one to another, and pray one for another, that ye may be healed. The effectual fervent prayer of a righteous man availeth much." (James 5:16, KJV)

Daily Thought:

Everyone is entitled to mistakes and misguiding. Don't beat yourself up. Instead, confess and apologize if the situation calls for it. Pray for yourself and others.

Prayer Starter:

Lord, I thank You for Your many blessings. Thank You for forgiving me and allowing me to "rest" in Your Word. I pray that I begin to build and rebuild relationships that are good to and for me. Give me strength to move forward.

. . .

Your Prayer:

Write your prayer here.

_____

_____

_____

_____

_____

DAY 8

Scripture(s):

"Let us therefore follow after the things which make for peace, and things wherewith one may edify another." (Romans 14:19, KJV)

Daily Thought:

We must build each other up, not tear each other down.

Prayer Starter:

Lord, I thank You that I am fearfully and wonderfully made. I ask that You protect my peace. I don't want to put myself in a position to be torn down mentally, emotionally, or physically. I pray that You will place the proper people in my life who will contribute to building me up.

Your Prayer:

Write your prayer here.

_____

_____

_____

_____

_____

Reflection Prompt:

What does the Bible say concerning those things that disturb your peace?

_____

_____

_____

_____

_____

DAY 9

Scripture(s):

"If there be therefore any consolation in Christ, if any comfort of love, if any fellowship of the Spirit, if any bowels and mercies, fulfil ye my joy, that ye be likeminded, having the same love, being of one accord, of one mind. Let nothing be done through strife or vainglory; but in lowliness of mind let each esteem other better than themselves. Look not every man on his own things, but every man also on the things of others." (Philippians 2:1–4, KJV)

Daily Thought:

Encourage someone today.

Prayer Starter:

Lord, I thank You for allowing me to share Your Word. I pray that I am not a stumbling block for myself or others. Help me to encourage and uplift with love and humility.

. . .

Your Prayer:

Write your prayer here.

_____

_____

_____

_____

_____

DAY 10

Scripture(s):

"Search me, O God, and know my heart: try me, and know my thoughts: and see if there be any wicked way in me, and lead me in the way everlasting." (Psalm 139:23–24, KJV)

Daily Thought:

Repeating and replaying situations and conversations is the enemy's plot to disturb your peace.

Prayer Starter:

Our Father who is in Heaven, thank You for Your daily provisions. Thank You for giving me a thirst for knowledge. I pray that You keep my mind free and clear from negative thoughts. Help me, O Lord, to not replay situations over in my mind but grant me wisdom and discernment to not make the same mistakes again.

. . .

Your Prayer:

Write your prayer here.

_____

_____

_____

_____

_____

Reflection Prompt:

What changes is God leading you to make concerning your peace?

_____

_____

_____

_____

_____

Now that you have completed one-third of this book, I pray that you are feeling renewed. You should have gained some insight into the things that have impacted your peace. Hopefully, you have accepted the fact that you must let go of some people and things that cannot be taken with you on this leg of your journey to find peace.

In the second half of this book, you will find the scripture and daily thought, but I am "taking the training wheels off" by eliminating the prayer starter. Now let's put what you have gained into action and deeper self-discovery!

DAY 11

Scripture(s):

"Walk in wisdom toward them that are without, redeeming the time. Let your speech be always with grace, seasoned with salt, that ye may know how ye ought to answer every man." (Colossians 4:5–6, KJV)

Scriptural Observation:

What do you observe about this scripture?

_____

_____

_____

_____

_____

Daily Application:

How can you apply this scripture to your daily life?

_____

_____

_____

_____

_____

Prayer:

Write your prayer here.

_____

_____

_____

_____

_____

DAY 12

Scripture(s):

"And this I pray, that your love may abound yet more and more in knowledge and in all judgment; that ye may approve things that are excellent; that ye may be sincere and without offence till the day of Christ." (Philippians 1:9–10, KJV)

Scriptural Observation:

What do you observe about this scripture?

_____

_____

_____

_____

_____

Daily Application:

How can you apply this scripture to your daily life?

_____

_____

_____

_____

_____

Prayer:

Write your prayer here.

_____

_____

_____

_____

_____

DAY 13

Scripture(s):

"Examine yourselves, whether ye be in the faith; prove your own selves. Know ye not your own selves, how that Jesus Christ is in you, except ye be reprobates?" (2 Corinthians 13:5, KJV)

Scriptural Observation:

What do you observe about this scripture?

_____

_____

_____

_____

_____

Daily Application:

How can you apply this scripture to your daily life?

_____
_____
_____
_____
_____

Prayer:

Write your prayer here.

_____
_____
_____
_____
_____

DAY 14

Scripture(s):

"Looking diligently lest any man fail of the grace of God; lest any root of bitterness springing up trouble you, and thereby many be defiled." (Hebrews 12:15, KJV)

Scriptural Observation:

What do you observe about this scripture?

_____

_____

_____

_____

_____

Daily Application:

How can you apply this scripture to your daily life?

_____

_____

_____

_____

_____

Prayer:

Write your prayer here.

_____

_____

_____

_____

_____

Reflection Prompt:

Character says a lot about you. What aspect(s) of your character is God revealing to you?

_____

_____

_____

_____

_____

DAY 15

Scripture(s):

"Therefore if any man be in Christ, he is a new creature: old things are passed away; behold, all things are become new." (2 Corinthians 5:17, KJV)

Scriptural Observation:

What do you observe about this scripture?

_____

_____

_____

_____

_____

Daily Application:

How can you apply this scripture to your daily life?

_____

_____

_____

_____

_____

Prayer:

Write your prayer here.

_____

_____

_____

_____

_____

DAY 16

Scripture(s):

"Peace be within thy walls, and prosperity within thy palaces." (Psalm 122:7, KJV)

Scriptural Observation:

What do you observe about this scripture?

_____

_____

_____

_____

_____

Daily Application:

How can you apply this scripture to your daily life?

_____

_____

_____

_____

_____

Prayer:

Write your prayer here.

_____

_____

_____

_____

_____

Reflection Prompt:

When do you feel closest to God?

_____

_____

_____

_____

_____

DAY 17

Scripture(s):

"Mark the perfect man, and behold the upright: for the end of that man is peace." (Psalm 37:37, KJV)

Scriptural Observation:

What do you observe about this scripture?

_____

_____

_____

_____

_____

Daily Application:

How can you apply this scripture to your daily life?

_____

_____

_____

_____

_____

Prayer:

Write your prayer here.

_____

_____

_____

_____

_____

DAY 18

Scripture(s):

"Heaviness in the heart of man maketh it stoop: but a good word maketh it glad." (Proverbs 12:25, KJV)

Scriptural Observation:

What do you observe about this scripture?

_____

_____

_____

_____

_____

Daily Application:

How can you apply this scripture to your daily life?

_____
_____
_____
_____
_____

Prayer:

Write your prayer here.

_____
_____
_____
_____
_____

Reflection Prompt:

Let's be honest. What are some things that you are grateful for?

_____
_____
_____
_____
_____

DAY 19

Scripture(s):

"Great peace have they which love thy law: and nothing shall offend them."
(Psalm 119:165, KJV)

Scriptural Observation:

What do you observe about this scripture?

_____

_____

_____

_____

_____

Daily Application:

How can you apply this scripture to your daily life?

_____

_____

_____

_____

_____

Prayer:

Write your prayer here.

_____

_____

_____

_____

_____

DAY 20

Scripture(s):

"And the same day, when the even was come, he saith unto them, Let us pass over unto the other side. And when they had sent away the multitude, they took him even as he was in the ship. And there were also with him other little ships.

And there arose a great storm of wind, and the waves beat into the ship, so that it was now full.

And he was in the hinder part of the ship, asleep on a pillow: and they awake him, and say unto him, Master, carest thou not that we perish?

And he arose, and rebuked the wind, and said unto the sea, Peace, be still. And the wind ceased, and there was a great calm.

And he said unto them, Why are ye so fearful? how is it that ye have no faith?

And they feared exceedingly, and said one to another, What manner of man is this, that even the wind and the sea obey him?" (Mark 4:35–41, KJV)

Scriptural Observation:

What do you observe about this scripture?

_____
_____
_____
_____
_____

Daily Application:

How can you apply this scripture to your daily life?

_____

_____

_____

_____

_____

Prayer:

Write your prayer here.

_____

_____

_____

_____

_____

ARE YOU BITTER AND DO YOU WANT TO BE BETTER?

Scripture Reference: Genesis 4:1–9 (KJV)

And Adam knew Eve his wife; and she conceived, and bare Cain, and said, I have gotten a man from the Lord.

And she again bare his brother Abel. And Abel was a keeper of sheep, but Cain was a tiller of the ground.

And in process of time it came to pass, that Cain brought of the fruit of the ground an offering unto the Lord.

And Abel, he also brought of the firstlings of his flock and of the fat thereof. And the Lord had respect unto Abel and to his offering:

But unto Cain and to his offering he had not respect. And Cain was very wroth, and his countenance fell.

And the Lord said unto Cain, Why art thou wroth? and why is thy countenance fallen?

If thou doest well, shalt thou not be accepted? and if thou doest not well, sin lieth at the door. And unto thee shall be his desire, and thou shalt rule over him.

And Cain talked with Abel his brother: and it came to pass, when they were in the field, that Cain rose up against Abel his brother, and slew him.

And the Lord said unto Cain, Where is Abel thy brother? And he said, I know not: Am I my brother's keeper?

The Bitter Root

The Bible tells us that Cain was born first, followed by Abel. Cain worked the soil, and Abel tended a flock. Both brought offerings to the Lord—Cain brought fruits of the soil, and Abel brought fat portions from the firstborn of his flock. The text also tells us that the Lord looked with favor on Abel and his offering but not on Cain and his.

You should also take note that Abel was a "stand-up guy"—he was good, righteous, and never did his brother wrong. Despite how he was treated, he was still respectful to Cain. Cain, on the other hand, was wicked, lived a bad life, and was worldly, so his sacrifice was seen as an abomination. The Lord did not respect Cain, and therefore, did not respect Cain's offering.

The Lord's favor toward Abel made Cain angry—so much so that the Lord saw it on his face and asked, *"Why are you angry?"* If you pay attention to the text, the Lord asked Cain a question He already knew the answer to. In essence: *Why are you sulking and throwing a tantrum?* The Lord also told Cain that if he did well—that is, if he did what he was supposed to do—he would be accepted. If not, *"sin lieth at the door,"* waiting for him.

What happened next? Cain said to Abel, *"Let me holla at you for a minute."*

He approached Abel in a friendly, unsuspecting manner and led him out to the field, where he attacked and killed him. Cain was familiar to Abel. Abel would not have suspected such a thing from his own blood—his own brother.

Isn't that how some folks are? When you begin the "glow-up," they stop "showing up." They become envious and may even believe they deserve the favor that you have. That's how Cain felt: *"I should be favored. I'm the firstborn."* Cain was upset because he was not seen as favorable in the Lord's eyes. I would even say that this made Cain bitter.

Bitterness is defined as anger and disappointment at being treated unfairly. Bitterness causes you to do and say sinful things.

Genesis 4:9–12 (KJV)

And the Lord said unto Cain, Where is Abel thy brother? And he said, I know not: Am I my brother's keeper?

And he said, What hast thou done? the voice of thy brother's blood crieth unto me from the ground.

And now art thou cursed from the earth, which hath opened her mouth to receive thy brother's blood from thy hand;

When thou tillest the ground, it shall not henceforth yield unto thee her strength; a fugitive and a vagabond shalt thou be in the earth.

Cain had been tried, convicted, and sentenced for murder.

Bitterness Blossomed

We have the seed of sin, which can birth another sin. The original sin of eating the forbidden fruit opened the door for sin to creep in. The bitterness in Cain took root and ultimately led him to murder his brother.

When sin entered the human race, it brought dysfunctional and fractured families. Is your family disrupting or disturbing your peace?

Think about it: when you are bitter, it is hard to be patient, humble, and kind. When you are bitter, it is hard to forgive and forget. Bitterness causes distress, unrest, and it disturbs our peace.

This is not the only time in the Bible where bitterness reared its head. In **2 Samuel 3:27,** Joab kissed Abner and then killed him. **Absalom** feasted with his brother Amnon and then killed him. In **2 Samuel 17:1–4,** Ahithophel plotted with Absalom to kill David.

The text tells us that Ahithophel was bitter and held a grudge against David. But what did David do? David had inquired about and committed adultery with Bathsheba, the daughter of Eliam and the wife of Uriah the Hittite. What we later find out is that Ahithophel was the grandfather of Bathsheba.

Ahithophel let his bitterness fester for ten years. He was a close friend and confidant of David, but David's act of adultery indirectly affected him. When you are bitter, instead of holding your friend accountable with love, you allow the enemy to get in your head—and then you make bad decisions.

Bitterness can be planted by envy, jealousy, wrongdoing, a relationship gone wrong, and more. But at its core, bitterness is rooted in pride. You harbor bitterness because you believe you deserve better.

Cain felt he deserved better. Ahithophel felt he deserved a better apology than what David gave. Most times you do deserve better, but when bitterness is buried under self-pity, it is a sign that the enemy already has your ear.

Cain began to pity himself. The Lord asked him, *"Why is your face sullen?"* God gave him a warning. Yet Cain wore his bitterness like a mask. We walk around pretending everything is all right, but people can see it all over our faces.

Cain's bitterness didn't just poison his spirit—it led him to physically murder his brother Abel.

Bitterness Personified

When we are bitter, we can be murderous with our words.

When we are bitter, we assassinate someone's character. We assassinate their integrity. We grow bitter when someone we know is focused on becoming a better version of themselves—while we feel stuck spinning our wheels.

Can you be happy for them, the person you call your friend?

We often use mid-life crises, stress, lack of sleep, or lack of peace as excuses for our behavior. But as believers in Christ, we are called to hold each other accountable. If I am my sister's keeper, I am not going to allow you to put yourself out there recklessly. I will not stand by and let you demean yourself.

We have a bond with one another, but we have a covenant with God.

One major difference between a bond and a covenant is this:

Our bond with others is *conditional*—based on feelings, offenses, or misunderstandings.

Our covenant with God is *unconditional*—sealed by His love, mercy, and grace.

Bitterness affects the bond. When you are bitter about a situation, you risk breaking bonds that God intended for accountability and growth.

But let me ask:

How can you hold someone accountable when you are walking

around looking like you've been sucking on a lemon—while trying to muster up a fake smile?

My friends and I have been upset with each other. There have been times when we didn't even talk. Part of that stems from someone holding the other accountable at the wrong time or in the wrong way. When someone holds your feet to the fire, you do not always take the correction well—sometimes you have to get upset first.

See, we couldn't stay bitter with each other and still hold each other accountable. We couldn't stay unforgiving either.

There are folks walking around the church holding grudges—unable to forgive. An unforgiving spirit hinders our worship and destroys our fellowship with God and with God's people. How can you freely worship God when you are harboring bitterness in your heart?

If you've ever seen the movie *Stomp the Yard*, there's a scene where Columbus Short's character is new to the college. He follows a girl across campus and tries to push through a fraternity's line to get to her.

Now, everybody on campus knows: you don't walk through a sorority or fraternity line. That is a sign of disrespect.

Every line has a line leader at the front and someone at the end (the "tail"). The leader watches what is ahead; the tail holds the line together and sees everything that the leader cannot see behind them.

When Columbus Short's character tries to push through, he gets roughed up and pushed back a few times.

He gets pushed to the side, and the president of the fraternity tells him, *"I don't know if you're crazy or dumb, but you don't want this smoke."* In so many words, he's warned to back off.

Columbus Short's character is like the enemy. He tries to outmaneuver you. He tries to fit in where he does not belong. He thinks he is smart, but he is ignorant.

However, if you have a weak link in your line—he's coming in!

Holding on to grudges is a weak link.

Unforgiveness is a weak link.

Jealousy is a weak link.

Envy is a weak link.

Bitterness is a weak link.

You cannot afford to be bitter.

You cannot afford to lose focus.

You cannot afford to stop holding your brothers and sisters accountable.

You cannot be bitter and still be your brother's keeper.

When you are bitter, you are not praying for the person you have a bond with.

Matthew 5:23–24 (KJV) says:

"Therefore if thou bring thy gift to the altar, and there rememberest that thy brother hath ought against thee; leave there thy gift before the altar, and go thy way; first be reconciled to thy brother, and then come and offer thy gift."

Cain had something against his brother—and something against the Lord—and yet he brought his offering without reconciliation. God tells us clearly: *Make amends. Fix it. Don't go to bed angry. Don't waste time. Do it as soon as possible.*

How Do You Get Rid of Bitterness to Gain Peace?

1. Evaluate yourself.

"Examine yourselves, whether ye be in the faith; prove your own selves. Know ye not your own selves, how that Jesus Christ is in you, except ye be reprobates?" (2 Corinthians 13:5, KJV)

If the Holy Spirit dwells within you, there should be no room for bitterness.

2. Repent.

Sometimes we claim to forgive but still harbor resentment, saying, *"I'll forgive, but I won't forget."*

That is not true forgiveness.

3. Help others heal.

"Looking diligently lest any man fail of the grace of God; lest any root of bitterness springing up trouble you, and thereby many be defiled." (Hebrews 12:15, KJV)

4. Obey Christ by giving forgiveness—even when you believe the person does not deserve it.

Bitterness is a weak link that allows the enemy to disrupt our peace.

To live in God's promise of peace, we must confront and release bitterness, embrace accountability, and extend forgiveness.

By doing so, we step into healing, restoration, and true spiritual growth.

Final Encouragement

You did it! You are two-thirds of the way finished. Keep pushing.

These sections were designed for **self-discovery** and **reflection**.

They were also meant to help you **pay closer attention** to those you call friends and to those you allow into your circle.

You have affirmed who God says you are. Healing and peace are near.

Get ready to "rest" in the newness that peace brings you.

You have reached the **final section** of this journal.

As you move forward:

• Read the scriptures carefully.

• Ask yourself: *What is this saying to me?*

• Are you ready to take action and live in the abundance of peace that God has promised you?

DAY 21

Scripture(s):

"And be not conformed to this world: but be ye transformed by the renewing of your mind, that ye may prove what is that good, and acceptable, and perfect, will of God." (Romans 12:2, KJV)

Daily Thought/Affirmation:

Your thoughts or affirmations here.

_____

_____

_____

_____

_____

Progress → What did you accomplish today?

Reflect here.

_____

_____

_____

_____

_____

Morning/Evening Prayer:

Write your prayer here.

_____

_____

_____

_____

_____

DAY 22

Scripture(s):

"And it came to pass after these things, that God did tempt Abraham, and said unto him, Abraham: and he said, Behold, here I am." (Genesis 22:1, KJV)

Daily Thought/Affirmation:

Your thoughts or affirmations here.

_____

_____

_____

_____

_____

Progress → What did you accomplish today?

Reflect here.

_____
_____
_____
_____
_____

Morning/Evening Prayer:

Write your prayer here.

_____
_____
_____
_____
_____

DAY 23

Scripture(s):

"And it came to pass after these things, that God did tempt Abraham, and said unto him, Abraham: and he said, Behold, here I am." (Genesis 22:1, KJV)

Daily Thought/Affirmation:

Your thoughts or affirmations here.

_____
_____
_____
_____
_____

Progress → What did you accomplish today?

Reflect here.

_____
_____
_____
_____
_____

Morning/Evening Prayer:

Write your prayer here.

_____
_____
_____
_____
_____

DAY 24

Scripture(s):

"And Hannah prayed, and said, My heart rejoiceth in the Lord, mine horn is exalted in the Lord: my mouth is enlarged over mine enemies; because I rejoice in thy salvation." (1 Samuel 2:1, KJV)

Daily Thought/Affirmation:

Your thoughts or affirmations here.

_____

_____

_____

_____

_____

Progress → What did you accomplish today?

Reflect here.

_____
_____
_____
_____
_____

Morning/Evening Prayer:

Write your prayer here.

_____
_____
_____
_____
_____

DAY 25

Scripture(s):

"And said, I beseech thee, O Lord God of heaven, the great and terrible God, that keepeth covenant and mercy for them that love him and observe his commandments:

Let thine ear now be attentive, and thine eyes open, that thou mayest hear the prayer of thy servant, which I pray before thee now, day and night, for the children of Israel thy servants, and confess the sins of the children of Israel, which we have sinned against thee: both I and my father's house have sinned." (Nehemiah 1:5–6, KJV)

Daily Thought/Affirmation:

Your thoughts or affirmations here.

_____

_____

_____

_____

_____

Progress → What did you accomplish today?

Reflect here.

_____
_____
_____
_____
_____

Morning/Evening Prayer:

Write your prayer here.

_____
_____
_____
_____
_____

DAY 26

Scripture(s):

"The Lord shall fight for you, and ye shall hold your peace." (Exodus 14:14, KJV)

Daily Thought/Affirmation:

Your thoughts or affirmations here.

_____

_____

_____

_____

_____

Progress → What did you accomplish today?

Reflect here.

_____

_____

_____

_____

_____

Morning/Evening Prayer:

Write your prayer here.

_____

_____

_____

_____

_____

DAY 27

Scripture(s):

"The Lord is with you, while ye be with him; and if ye seek him, he will be found of you; but if ye forsake him, he will forsake you." (2 Chronicles 15:2a, KJV)

Daily Thought/Affirmation:

Your thoughts or affirmations here.

_____

_____

_____

_____

_____

Progress → What did you accomplish today?

Reflect here.

_____
_____
_____
_____
_____

Morning/Evening Prayer:

Write your prayer here.

_____
_____
_____
_____

DAY 28

Scripture(s):

"Then I told them of the hand of my God which was good upon me; as also the king's words that he had spoken unto me." (Nehemiah 2:18, KJV)

Daily Thought/Affirmation:

Your thoughts or affirmations here.

_____

_____

_____

_____

_____

Progress → What did you accomplish today?

Reflect here.

_____
_____
_____
_____
_____

Morning/Evening Prayer:

Write your prayer here.

_____
_____
_____
_____
_____

DAY 29

Scripture(s):

"These things I have spoken unto you, that in me ye might have peace. In the world ye shall have tribulation: but be of good cheer; I have overcome the world." (John 16:33, KJV)

Daily Thought/Affirmation:

Your thoughts or affirmations here.

_____
_____
_____
_____
_____

Progress → What did you accomplish today?

Reflect here.

Morning/Evening Prayer:

Write your prayer here.

DAY 30

Scripture(s):

"Now the Lord of peace himself give you peace always by all means. The Lord be with you all." (2 Thessalonians 3:16, KJV)

Daily Thought/Affirmation:

Your thoughts or affirmations here.

_____
_____
_____
_____
_____

Progress → What did you accomplish today?

Reflect here.

_____
_____
_____
_____
_____

Morning/Evening Prayer:

Write your prayer here.

_____
_____
_____
_____
_____

NOW IS THE TIME

Then I said,

*"Lord, the God of heaven, the great and awesome God, who keeps His covenant of love with those who love Him and keep His commandments, let Your ear be attentive and Your eyes open to hear the prayer Your servant is praying before You day and night for Your servants, the people of Israel. I confess the sins we Israelites, including myself and my father's family, have committed against You. We have acted very wickedly toward You. We have not obeyed the commands, decrees, and laws You gave Your servant Moses.

Remember the instruction You gave Your servant Moses, saying, 'If you are unfaithful, I will scatter you among the nations, but if you return to Me and obey My commands, then even if your exiled people are at the farthest horizon, I will gather them from there and bring them to the place I have chosen as a dwelling for My Name.'

They are Your servants and Your people, whom You redeemed by Your great strength and Your mighty hand. Lord, let Your ear be attentive to the prayer of this Your servant and to the prayer of Your servants who delight in revering Your name. Give Your servant

success today by granting him favor in the presence of this man."*
(Nehemiah 1:5–11, NIV)

"I was cupbearer to the king." (Nehemiah 1:11, NIV)

Much like Ezra, Nehemiah emerged from a similar background and
circumstance. Nehemiah had gotten word that his city was in ruin.
The Jewish remnants who survived the exile were in great trouble.
The wall was broken down, and the gates had been burned with fire
(Nehemiah 1:3).

This meant the living conditions were horrible and showed signs of
poverty and slavery. It left the people exposed to their enemies.

This came about fifteen years after Ezra had received a similar word
—that the people again had fallen into sin, even though the temple
had been rebuilt (Ezra 9:1–2). Both Ezra and Nehemiah went to their
respective kings to ask permission to return to their cities to rebuild.

Nehemiah was the cupbearer to his king—a trusted advisor and a
high-ranking Persian official. His status is important because he
didn't think he was so high that he couldn't empathize with his
people, nor was he ashamed to be related to them.

The cupbearer was also the one who tested and served beverages to
the king to ensure they weren't poisoned by his enemies. Each time
Nehemiah served, he risked his life for the king.

One day, when Nehemiah was taking wine to the king, the king asked
him, *"Why does your face look so sad when you are not ill? This can be
nothing but sadness of the heart."* (Nehemiah 2:2, NIV)

Nehemiah was afraid to respond but found favor with the king.
Gathering his courage, he asked for permission to go to Jerusalem to
rebuild the wall (Nehemiah 2:4–5). After meeting with the king,
Nehemiah was granted permission to go (Nehemiah 2:8).

In verses 5–11, Nehemiah gives us a prescription for prayer. Upon
hearing the news, Nehemiah:

1. **Weeps and mourns** — not just when he heard the news, but for days (Nehemiah 1:4).
2. **Fasts and prays** — not in public, but before God in heaven, who sees in secret and rewards openly (Matthew 6:6, 18).
3. **Reminds God who He is and His covenant** — he tells God, *"You are great, You are awesome, You are a mighty God!"* (Nehemiah 1:5).
4. **Confesses his and Israel's sins** — repentance (Nehemiah 1:6–7).

Ezra follows this same prescription in **Ezra 7:27–28**:

"Praise be to the Lord, the God of our ancestors, who has put it into the king's heart to bring honor to the house of the Lord in Jerusalem in this way and who has extended His good favor to me before the king and his advisers and all the king's powerful officials. Because the hand of the Lord my God was on me, I took courage and gathered leaders from Israel to go up with me." (NIV)

In **Ezra 9:3–15**, Ezra prays a heartfelt prayer of confession, repentance, and asks for forgiveness.

This prescription that both Nehemiah and Ezra use shows us that we must humble ourselves before God and acknowledge who He is—recognizing not only His power, but also His love for us.

Following this prescription helps strengthen your relationship with God.

And when you begin to do this consistently, you will experience breakthroughs and miracles just as Ezra and Nehemiah did.

Nehemiah gathered materials and selected a few skilled men. These skilled men were officers of the army and cavalry who would escort him to Jerusalem (Nehemiah 2:9).

Nehemiah 2:16–18 (NIV):

"The officials did not know where I had gone or what I was doing, because as yet I had said nothing to the Jews or the priests or nobles or officials or any others who would be doing the work. Then I said to them, 'You see the trouble we are in: Jerusalem lies in ruins, and its gates have been burned with fire. Come, let us rebuild the wall of Jerusalem, and we will no longer be in disgrace.' I also told them about the gracious hand of my God on me and what the king had said to me."

They replied, "Let us start rebuilding." So they began this good work.

Now is the time to stop telling everyone your plans.

There are moments when you cannot let people know what you are doing.

Not everyone will be happy for you. Not everyone will be willing to help you.

There will come a time when you must gather your select few and say, *"Come with me."*

Nehemiah didn't seek outside counsel first—he went directly to God in prayer!

Now is the time to start with prayer first.

Now is the time to follow Nehemiah's prescription!

By Chapter 4, Sanballat, Tobiah, and other enemies were getting upset because the wall was being rebuilt. They laughed at the workers and even said that if a fox jumped on the wall, it would collapse (Nehemiah 4:3). They were angry and tried to rise up against them. But Nehemiah and his team had God on their side.

There is always someone who will try to minimize or discourage you when you are attempting to dig yourself out of a sunken place—a pit, if you will. When you are trying to re-establish your reputation, your career, or your business—or when you have been to jail and are trying to re-enter society—you may even just be trying to get your "snap back."

People see you changing your life. You are in the middle of a "glow-up." You are being blessed, and your enemies see it. They try to discredit you, talk about you, and remind others of your "used to be."

We should be like Nehemiah. Even with all the threats, the plots and schemes, and the negativity, Nehemiah continued to do the good work that God had put on his heart (Nehemiah 2:18; Nehemiah 6:3).

Much like Ezra and Nehemiah, Mordecai mourned deeply. He tore his clothes, put on sackcloth and ashes, and fasted, weeping bitterly (Esther 4:1–3).

Mordecai told Queen Esther,

"Do not think that because you are in the king's house you alone of all the Jews will escape.

For if you remain silent at this time, relief and deliverance for the Jews will arise from another place, but you and your father's family will perish.

And who knows but that you have come to your royal position for such a time as this?" (Esther 4:13–14, NIV)

Queen Esther, much like Nehemiah, chose to risk her life for the sake of her people.

I'm sure many of us have flown before. As you taxi down the runway, the flight crew goes over the emergency protocols. They tell you that oxygen masks will fall from the overhead compartment in case of emergency. They instruct you to *"put on your own mask first before assisting others."*

Nehemiah had to get right first:

1. He wept, mourned, and fasted—a spiritual detox (Nehemiah 1:4).
2. He gave God all the honor and praise (Nehemiah 1:5).
3. He repented not only for himself but for his father's people (Nehemiah 1:6–7).

He did all of that before he went to the king and before he journeyed to Jerusalem.

Likewise, Queen Esther spent twelve months preparing to become queen (Esther 2:12). She built trust with the king before she could go to him on behalf of her people.

Now is the time!
You have wept.
You have mourned.
You have fasted.

Now is the time!

Now is the time for you to rid yourself of whatever is holding you back from the plan and the purpose God has for your life!

Nehemiah, Ezra, and Queen Esther each demonstrate that true peace comes from seeking God first before taking action.

Their stories reveal that peace is not the absence of challenges, but the confidence that comes from trusting in God's plan.

• Nehemiah sought peace with God first through humility, confession, and praise. His actions reflected an inner peace that came from trusting in God's covenant and aligning his mission with God's will.

• Ezra sought God through prayer and fasting, acknowledging the sins of Israel and asking for God's guidance. His faith led to restoration and revival, showing that peace comes through humility and obedience to God's word.

• Queen Esther found peace in trusting God even when risking her life. She fasted and sought God's favor before approaching the king, showing that peace is rooted in surrendering to God's will, even in dangerous situations.

Congratulations!

You have come to the end of this journal.

I pray that you are on the road to healing and are making peace a priority in your life. Now is the time to walk in peace and purpose without distractions.

Trials will come to test your faith. But the Bible reminds us in 1 **Peter 1:7**:

"So that the proof of your faith, being more precious than gold which perishes though tested by fire, may be found to result in praise, glory, and honor at the revelation of Jesus Christ." (NASB)

Final Prayer

Lord, we thank You for the reader and their willingness to invite You into their life.

We thank You for this, their time of self-reflection.

We ask that You bless them with Your wisdom, courage, patience, and peace.

We ask that they are renewed—mind, body, and spirit.

May You guide their steps and fill their hearts with peace and perseverance as they embark on this journey.

We pray for their growth. Surround them with Your love, strength, and protection.

In the name of Jesus, Amen.

ABOUT THE AUTHOR

The author is a licensed and ordained minister at the Rose of Sharon C.O.G. in Cleveland, Ohio. In addition to preaching, Dr. Hughley is currently the Singles Ministry Leader and has held Youth Ministry Co-Leader and Advisor for the youth flag team offices. Dr. Hughley is an Elementary School Principal, a published author, member of the National Sorority of Phi Delta Kappa, Inc. Alpha Xi Chapter and Life member of Sigma Gamma Rho Sorority, Inc. She is the dog mom to Phoenix and Harlem.

instagram.com/itslikefree0

www.ingramcontent.com/pod-product-compliance
Lightning Source LLC
Chambersburg PA
CBHW071103120626
46546CB00003B/1259